FALLACIES OF EVOLUTION

To My Father
A. J. HOOVER

CONTENTS

PREFACE

I have followed the creation/evolution controversy for several years now. I even participated in it briefly when I debated Berkeley scientist Dr. Dick Lemmons on TV. During this time I have seen the need for a small book explaining the issues to the layman. I noticed how easy it was for the scientist to intimidate the layman with complicated talk about homology, geology, paleontology, and genetics.

Part of my purpose in this short essay is to cut through the verbiage and jargon of the "experts" and encourage the average citizen to participate in this vital discussion. I want to defuse the argument that says, "Let the scientists settle this question."

There is much evidence that we are living in a watershed of world history.[1] If so, what we do at this

1. See chapter 8 on the "New Consciousness," James W. Sire, *The Universe Next Door: A Basic World View Catalog* (Downers Grove, Ill.: InterVarsity Press, 1976).

critical juncture may affect many generations to come. Jesus criticized those who knew a lot about empirical science but weren't able to interpret the "signs of the times" (Matt. 16:1-4). The active participation of citizens with creationist convictions could have a profound impact on the way origins is taught in our public schools for years to come. If this work stimulates such interest and participation, I will consider my labor rewarded.

I am grateful to Dr. J. D. Thomas of the Biblical Research Press, Abilene, Texas, for permission to use some material from my books, *Fallacies of Unbelief* and *Ideas and Their Consequences*.

Arlie J. Hoover

Chapter 1

INTRODUCTION

"Let me see the hands of all those who believe in that stupid theory of creation!"

This is how a certain evolutionist started out his semester class in biology one fall morning. Do you think it's very fair to begin a class this way? Is it academic? Would it develop an open mind in the students?

No, you say? Well, you're right. It's very bad form for a teacher to intimidate a student and prejudice his mind against any theory—no matter what field he's in. By calling creation "stupid" this biology teacher committed a logical fallacy called "Poisoning the Wells," which is discrediting a source of evidence before you even consider it. It would be like a defense attorney in court saying to the jury, "My client must be innocent because all the witnesses about to speak against him are liars." Any jury would disregard such a remark.

Evolutionists have been intimidating people in this way for decades now and I think it's time we put a stop to it. I've written this little book in hopes that the public will rise up and demand equity in the teaching of origins.

Before you react, remember this point: I'm arguing a case for science, not for religion. This may sound strange, since the title of this book sounds like I'm against science. The fact is, I strongly believe in the scientific method, employed in its proper sphere. I think it is an admirable process for finding truth about the physical, empirical world. And one of the finest things about the scientific method is the rigorous standard of proof it demands of all its theories. I'm asking that we apply that same rigorous standard of proof to the theory of evolution and see if it can take it.

My basic premise in this essay is simple: the problem of origins is either an open question or a closed question. If it's a closed question, I'd like to know who closed it. Who said it was closed? When did someone close it? What authority has determined that the question of origins is closed?

On the other hand, if origins is still an open question, then we dare not teach only one theory of origins and prejudice the minds of our students. That would mean that we just happen to teach what the stronger group can force us to teach. Our educational philosophy then becomes merely, "Might makes right!" We are then no better than Nazi Germany or Soviet Russia in our educational philosophy.

In their zeal to prove that evolution is "the only scientific theory of origins," evolutionists commit several fallacies—logical errors that scholarly, rational men really shouldn't commit. Pointing out these fallacies doesn't necessarily discredit the theory of evolution; it just shows that evolution hasn't established itself as the *only* theory of origins. Evolution should move over and allow creation to be considered as a possible theory of origins.

I'm certainly not advocating that we kick evolution out of science classes. Nor am I for reintroducing creation in the classes as the only possible theory. However, I do feel that to be consistent we must either teach both creation and evolution or teach neither. Certainly, if origins is still an open question, then it would be unjust to teach only one theory of origins.

Chapter 2

FALLACIES OF SCIENTISM

We need a little historical background to understand some of the fallacies evolutionists commit. We seem to be living in a strategic period these days. Up through the 1950s science was almost a sacred cow, a hallowed institution. Since the 1960s, however, there has been a refreshing resurgence of interest in the metaphysical, the supernatural, the supersensible. People are no longer ashamed to affirm that they believe in something "beyond" the empirical senses.

Many books have appeared in recent years stressing the limitations of the empirical scientific method and attacking the arrogant attitudes of the past. It's hard to shake off the old thought patterns in just a few years, however, and we still find people who have the "scientific reflex." In this chapter we'll look at various fallacies evolutionists committed during this recent period when science was so powerful that none dared challenge it for fear of appearing old-fashioned.

THE FALLACY OF SCIENTISM

The word *scientism* has been used for a long time to mean an uncritical worship of the empirical scientific method, an excessive veneration of laboratory technique. To a person who commits this error, "science" is a sacred word, and the phrase, "Science has proved," has the force of a papal bull. To such people science has become a religion.

Thinkers who commit this fallacy urge us to "study the concrete, empirical, tangible world." They say, "Avoid the unseen, spiritual, metaphysical world, because that world doesn't really exist." This advice seems harmless at first, but after years of applying this method we discover that scientism destroys the recognition of all abstract things—like mind, values, morality, beauty, God. We're now living in the "hangover period," in the grisly morning-after of scientism, when all the bad consequences of such an approach become evident. It's time that all thinking citizens rise up and question the basic assumption of scientism: that all true knowledge is empirical, that all judgments are merely factual.

Ask yourself this question: "Why did scientists so easily reject non-empirical data, subjective factors, emotions, feelings, and values from their investigations?" These things seem very real to most people—

why were they ignored? The answer seems to be . . . simply because it was convenient! Scientists found it expedient to ignore these things, to *select* from the whole of experience only those elements that could be weighed, measured, numbered, or which lent themselves to mathematical treatment.

Scientists, therefore, committed the *Reductive Fallacy*. You commit this logical error when you "reduce" something complex down to something very simple, when you say, *"This is nothing but . . ."* and then zero in on a limited aspect of the total phenomenon. For example, you commit the reductive fallacy when you say things like: love is nothing but sex, man is nothing but an animal, music is nothing but sound, physics is nothing but mathematics. A music critic once quipped that a Beethoven string quartet was "nothing but horse hair scraping on cat's gut."

Scientism reduced all reality to the mere empirical world. By using this technique of reduction, simplification, and abstraction, the scientist succeeded to an astonishing degree in understanding and controlling the physical environment. In fact, it was the amazing success of practical science, the "wonders" of science, that made this reduction seem so plausible to many people. But this success was so intoxicating that many thinkers jumped to the conclusion that this useful abstraction from reality was reality itself. In sum, the great error of scientism was to identify the world of empirical science (a world from which all meaning and value had been deliberately excluded) with ultimate reality. This was probably history's most tragic case of "selective perception" or "tunnel vision."

Sir Arthur Eddington, a British scientist, used a good analogy to illustrate the fallacy of scientism. It seems there was a fisherman who concluded from his fishing experiments with a special net that "No creature of the sea is less than two inches long." This generalization disturbed some of his colleagues and they objected, arguing that many sea creatures were certainly less than two inches long, and they just slipped through the holes in the special net. But the fisherman was unmoved. "What my net can't catch ain't fish," he pontificated, and then he scornfully accused his detractors of having pre-scientific, medieval, metaphysical prejudices.

The scientist who refuses to believe in something he can't catch with his empirical senses is like this fisherman. Spiritual things like God, mind, freedom, morality, and beauty just slip through his net.

The theory of evolution enjoyed an unchallenged reign during the heyday of scientism because the "First and Great Commandment" was, "Thou shalt not postulate unseen entities." As long as the game was rigged to keep out metaphysical players, creation never had a chance. Evolution was king of origins and no other heir to the throne was allowed to exist. It's no wonder, then, that in recent years the demise of scientism is accompanied by a revival of interest in creation.

Let's now look at some characteristic fallacies that easily occur in a period of scientism.

MISUSE OF AUTHORITY

All of us find it necessary, from time to time, to appeal to an authority or an expert to prove something we believe. There is nothing wrong with citing a competent authority to prove something—if you don't break certain rules. Misuse of authority occurs when you break two basic rules about using experts.

(1) First, you can't use an expert to prove something unrelated to his field of competence. An expert on Renaissance art is not equipped to help you with your nutrition problems. No man can be an expert on every topic. Some men are world authorities in a limited field and faddists in other fields. Some Nobel Prize winners prove to be poorly informed in any fields outside of their specialization.

Yet many evolutionists think that all they have to do to prove evolution is to parrot the old cliché, "most scientists believe in evolution." In the first place, most of the scientists mentioned in the cliché aren't even in the fields related to evolution. Many of them wouldn't even know how to begin an argument for evolution.

In the second place, the cliché may be false, or at least exaggerated. Many scientists believe in creation. "Most" can mean anything from 51 percent to 99 percent and we have no way of knowing where the "most" falls. Even if you could determine that over 51 percent of scientists believe in evolution it wouldn't prove anything to a rational man. Is anyone seriously suggesting that a poll of scientists is a valid criterion for scientific truth? That would be the Gallup/Harris method, not the scientific method. As far as I can determine, counting noses has no part of the scientific method.

Ask yourself: "Has there ever been a time in the history of science when a widely-held position was given up by scientists?" Yes, most certainly. One obvious case would be in the last century when *most* scientists before Darwin held to creation and then changed to evolution. You could easily have argued in the year 1860 that, "Most scientists believe in creation, so evolution must be wrong."

An intellectual historian could cite many more examples of this phenomenon:

(a) What could you prove with a poll of scientists from Nazi Germany's Third Reich on the question of race?

(b) What could you prove from a poll of scientists in Stalin's Russia on the question of Marxism?

(c) What could you prove from a poll of physicists on the question of ether before the twentieth century?

(d) What could you prove from a poll of learned men in the Middle Ages on the shape of the earth?

We could list examples like this for several pages, but the point is simply that we should be careful not to deify the current opinion on *anything*. Learned people have held strongly to certain theories in the past that turned out to be false. *Any question is still an open question until adequate evidence has definitely closed it.* That's why I say that the statement, "Most scientists believe in evolution" is irrelevant, even if it is accurate.

(2) An even subtler misuse of authority occurs when you cite an expert on an issue—even if the issue is in his field—and you then assume that his judgment is infallible. Don't forget that your expert is still human, finite, and subject to error. Many experts can amass a mountain of facts on a certain topic but fail to relate the facts properly, or fail to draw the proper inferences from them. Those who are good at collecting data aren't always good at sorting it. Sometimes a high school student can detect an error in inference made by an expert.

Often we hear this complaint from evolutionists: "Why don't you just let the scientists decide?" The answer to this is obvious: We shouldn't let anyone do our thinking for us on such a vital problem as origins. To let the naturalistic scientist decide this matter would be like someone on the jury saying, "Why not let the District Attorney decide if the facts really prove the defendant guilty?" I think the defense attorney would object! The man who collects the facts has no inalienable right to fix his authoritative interpretation on the facts.

Strictly speaking, regardless of what the popular

cliché says, facts—whether in court or in science—never "speak for themselves." Facts speak *through* an interpreter *for* a theory. All facts, from all areas, must be organized, synthesized, and interpreted. And if you allow the man collecting the facts to also fix his authoritative interpretation on the facts, you are elevating scientists to the status of clergy. It often happens that an expert draws unwarranted conclusions from the facts he so expertly collects. Furthermore, a non-expert can often detect an error of inference made by an expert.

That's why in a court of law we use the "Adversary System." We have *two* attorneys to allow for cross-examination of the data. We permit *two* competing interpretations to battle it out and see which is a better interpretation of the data. In addition, we have a judge, who may not be an expert on the data, but who knows the rules of evidence and the canons of court procedure. We allow no dogmatizing and pontification in court.

Shouldn't it be the same in science? Any generally educated man has a right to inquire about the evidence behind the theory of evolution, even though he may not be an expert in biology, paleontology, or genetics. The rules of logic and the canons of evidence are common to several academic disciplines and no one has a monopoly on their right use. The question isn't, "What do scientists believe?" but "What is the evidence for the theory, regardless of what anyone believes?"

For example, it wouldn't bother me a bit if a scientist were to come over into my field (history) and challenge some widely-held thesis, such as, say, the Turner Thesis in American history or the Weber Thesis in European history. I certainly wouldn't say, "Get out of my field, you meddling scientist!" History isn't a closed shop. Rather, I would say, "Welcome, let's discuss this issue, and, by the way, what is your evidence?"

I should hope that this same open attitude would be practiced by all scientists concerning the theory of evolution. The only alternative I can see to this open attitude would be a closed shop, a kind of priestly system where a Pope of Science or an Archbishop of Evolution hands down infallible pronouncements on the data. It'll be a bad day for science if this takes place.

ARGUMENTUM AD POPULUM

Similar to misuse of authority is a fallacy called *Argumentum ad Populum*, an argument addressed "to the people." You commit this fallacy when you pander to popular feelings, when you tell your listeners what they want to hear rather than the unpleasant truth. We might also call this the "misuse of democracy." The majority thinks this is true, therefore it is true. The majority is doing this thing, therefore it should be done. The majority thinks this is valuable, therefore it is valuable.

As noted earlier, what the majority believes is no sure criterion for truth. When one argues this way on evolution, he not only misuses authority but also commits the *Argumentum ad Populum* fallacy. Friedrich Nietzsche hit the nail on the head when he said that "public opinion" may be the same as "private laziness." No rational thinker should ever allow the public, the majority, to do his thinking for him, especially in this crucial realm of origins.

Many people argue for evolution and against creation by claiming that evolution is the "scientific," "modern," "educated," or "progressive" view of origins. One such individual told me that "only a small minority of rednecked Bible-bangers want to go back to medieval times and keep evolution out of the schools." (This man committed yet another fallacy in this statement: the Misuse of Emotional Terms. Words like *rednecked* and *Bible-banger* are designed to cloud the issue emotionally, not contribute to clear thought).

CHRONOLOGICAL SNOBBERY

One of the easiest fallacies for modern man to commit is "Chronological Snobbery," a term coined by the late C. S. Lewis. You commit it when you refute something merely by dating it, usually dating it very old. We could coin a Latin phrase ourselves and call it *Argumentum ab Annis*, "argument because of age." People who commit Chronological Snobbery usually employ some temporal adjective to put down an idea, such as "Victorian," "medieval," "primitive," "pre-scientific," or "ante-deluvian." They are quick to say that something is "out of date."

Evolutionists sometimes argue that since evolution is the "current" or "modern" or "latest" view of origins it is therefore superior to creation. We need to remind them that evolution is rather old itself. You can trace it back to the sixth century B. C., to classical Greece. Even if it were the younger of the two theories, however, that wouldn't prove anything. Age isn't a standard for truth either way, young or old. Some very old ideas are still true and some very modern ideas are false—and vice versa. You don't refute a theory simply by dating it.

One excellent historical example of this occurred during the Age of Enlightenment. Twentieth-century philosophers and scientists marvel at how one eminent German thinker, Gottfried Wilhelm von Leibnitz (1646-1716), anticipated the modern conception of nature as energy, rather than as discrete material particles. Leibnitz's world view lost out in the eighteenth century, however, because the popular Newtonian world view suited the social needs of the time better. As one intellectual history text says:

> The pragmatic and psychological needs of the eighteenth century obscured these limitations of the Newtonian world-view . . . and it became the new orthodoxy of the age on the basis of its successes in physics, sustaining with imperturbable calm all assaults upon its sublime regularity for more than 150 years. It alone seemed

capable of providing the substructure upon which could be raised a civilization characterized by unlimited confidence in man and the hope of an ever more brilliant future for humanity. Its very simplicity was its own best credential, and its practical results amply justified the confidence placed in it. Therefore, Newton was enshrined in the sanctuary of Voltaire's *Letters concerning the English Nation* and Pope's *Essay on Man,* while Leibniz was laughed off the philosophical stage to the accompaniment of quotations from *Candide.* The victory of Newtonianism in popular culture, however, represented in many respects the triumph of the simple over the complicated.[1]

Thinkers who preferred the Newtonian world view disliked the Leibnitzian world view because it too closely resembled the magico-mystical view of the Middle Ages, the view that was considered too old-fashioned for educated people of the Enlightenment. How ironic that the "medieval" view of Leibnitz has come back in the twentieth century! This case is a clear warning against the dangers of Chronological Snobbery.

CONCLUSION

These three fallacies—Misuse of Authority, *Argumentum ad Populum,* and Chronological Snobbery—were very prevalent in the recent era of arrogant scientism. Now that scientism is on the wane, the evolutionist must produce *evidence* for his

---

1. Coates, W. H., et al, *The Emergence of Liberal Humanism* (New York: McGraw Hill, 1966) 1:266.

theory. He can no longer appeal to popular sentiments, or to age, or to the majority opinion of scientists or laymen to justify teaching evolution as the
only theory of origins. In the next chapter we'll look
at the evidence offered for the theory of evolution.

Chapter 3

SPECIAL PLEADING

Is there any evidence for evolution? Well, of course there is! You couldn't explain why thousands of people for more than a century have believed in evolution unless there were *some* evidence for it.

But is the evidence strong enough? That's the crucial question. The District Attorney may have enough evidence to convince the Grand Jury that a trial must be held, but in the final trial his evidence may fail to convict the defendant "beyond reasonable doubt." It's vital, therefore, that we attempt to evaluate the strength of the evidence for evolution.

The evidence must be particularly strong if evolution is the only view of origins we teach in the public schools. By teaching it as the only view, teachers are saying, in effect, "This is the only view of origins certain enough to pass on to posterity." Many evolutionists claim that evolution is "the only scientific view of origins" or "the only theory that can be empirically verified" and hence, the only one that we should teach in science classes. Some admit that it might be all right to "mention" creation in social studies classes.

THE FALLACY OF SPECIAL PLEADING

I maintain that the evidence for evolution is not strong enough for the evolutionist to claim that it is "the only plausible view of origins." I maintain that the evidence is good enough to establish evolution as one possible theory of origins, but not good enough to teach it in the public schools as the *only* theory of origins.

In other words, I accuse the evolutionist of the *Fallacy of Special Pleading*. You commit this fallacy when you dramatize the material that favors your position and ignore or belittle the material that weighs against your position. A good illustration of special pleading is the landlord who proved to the building inspector that he was providing enough heat for an apartment he owned—but he hung the thermometer on the radiator instead of on the wall.

If we now look at the various lines of evidence for the theory of evolution we'll find that the model (or system) of creation can explain the data just as well as evolution—perhaps better in some cases.

(1) **Comparative anatomy** supposedly proves that

similar animals have a common ancestry. One can easily see an analogy between nails and hoofs, hands and claws, fish scales and bird feathers. There is certainly a striking structural similarity between a bat's wing, a man's arm, and a whale's flipper. This seems a cogent argument for evolution until we raise the simple question: does structural similarity demand genetic relationship?

How do you know for sure that a Creator-Designer wouldn't also come up with similar structures? Since the laws of motion, aerodynamics, and hydrodynamics are the same all over the earth, wouldn't it be reasonable to suppose that a Designer would make wings that resemble arms, scales that resemble feathers, arms that resemble flippers, and nails that resemble hoofs?

For instance, a ship, a bridge, and an office building resemble each other because they all have steel girders, but this doesn't prove they have a genetic relationship. It could just as well prove that they all were made by the same architect, who, in all three cases, needed a certain structure for a certain function.

For a long time evolutionists have been plotting charts of the "similar" features of animals—skeletons, appendages, embryos, protein, and blood. They have constructed impressive "ladders of animal life" to show the (alleged) orderly progression from simple to complex. But all this imaginary reconstruction rests on the assumption that the degree of similarity be-

tween two animals describes their degree of relationship. This is merely an assumption; it has no real
scientific basis. For example, the myna bird and the
parrot can mimick human speech very well, but this
doesn't make them our relatives. An albino human
being and an albino deer obviously didn't get their
albinism from a common ancestor.

In recent years, furthermore, many biologists have
complained that our entire classification system is
filled with arbitrary distinctions between animals. We
often find similarities that prove the wrong relationship. For example, the platypus of Australia has some
features like a duck—webbed feet, tarsal spurs, and a
duck-like bill. Yet zoologists say its relationship to
the duck is quite distant. They tell us that these similarities are only superficial. But if this is so, isn't it
possible that some of the highly touted similarities
used as evidence for descent are also superficial?

(2) **Comparative embryology** seems to support
evolution. The embryos of many animals, including
man, do resemble each other at early stages. Evolutionists used to claim that man in the course of his
embryonic development repeats the evolutionary
history of the phylum to which he belongs. The most
frequently-cited example of this is the so-called gill
slits, or bronchial grooves, and gill arches, found in
the human throat, said to resemble the gill slits and
gill arches of a fish.

But here again, the argument depends on a rather

fanciful and arbitrary system of comparisons. It is easy to find a number of superficial resemblances in animal embryos when there are so many hundreds of possible features to compare.

Moreover, a little reflection will show that the thesis of evolution isn't at all necessary to explain most embryonic similarities. If a man starts out as a single cell it's because that is exactly what you would expect if he grows in the womb from simple to complex. You needn't suggest that he was once a one-celled animal to explain that fact. If his heart is at first a single pulsating tube, like that of an earthworm, it's because that's all his circulatory system needs in the early stages of growth.

Another telling point is that these similar structures rarely function in the way the organs they resemble are supposed to function. For example, if human gill slits recapitulate the fish stage, they should function as respirators, but they don't.

(3) **Vestigial organs** such as the appendix, the caecum, and the tonsils in man are often cited as proof of evolution. These organs, it is argued, were once functional but lost their usefulness and gradually deteriorated. Certain flightless birds, such as the kiwi and the ostrich, have useless wings that are said to be vestigial.

This evidence is very weak. The creation model can easily incorporate a concept of "decaying organs" into its network of assumptions. There is nothing about vestigial organs that demands evolution. Furthermore, it's quite possible that many organs have a function we haven't yet discovered. Doctors are by no means universally agreed that the appendix is useless, and cells of the tonsils produce helpful antibodies.

(4) **Artificial breeding** is often used as proof of evolution. For example, man probably developed the dog through a domestication of the wolf. Luther Burbank developed the Idaho potato by selective breeding. Thus some people reason: isn't it possible that nature might have produced over long ages what man has done recently with deliberate foresight?

Yes, certainly it's possible, but this is not scientific evidence, because the two cases aren't really parallel. You can't go from what man has done by deliberate and rational choice to what nature has—allegedly—done by blind, accidental variations. You need more evidence than just the fact that man has produced some variations in animal and plant types. For example, we could probably produce a pyramid, even one the size of Khufu's, with modern technology, but that wouldn't prove anything about how the Egyptians did it 5000 years ago. How *we* did it is no necessary proof of how *they* did it.

Furthermore, most of the variations produced by man so far are rather limited, capable of falling into the two lowest classes on the scale: species and genus. In his *Origin of Species* Darwin made a great deal of the finches on Galapagos Islands, which are remarkably varied in several ways. But despite all the variations, they are still just finches; the variations never produce a new species or genus.

Some of the most striking animal variations, like the mule, are sterile, which doesn't help the theory of evolution very much. If the theory is to get any help from this argument you need a genuinely *new kind* of animal that can reproduce normally after its kind.

Since we've touched on this problem of a *new kind* of animal, let me note that Bible scholars are unsure exactly what was meant by the word "kind" (Hebrew: *min)* in the first chapter of Genesis. It could have meant species, or genus, or family. Many creationists admit the possibility of a limited or "micro" evolution, that is, they grant that mutations or variations are possible on the lower levels of the classification scale. The animal classes go like this from the most general down to the most specific:

Kingdom
Phylum
Class
Order
Family ⎫
Genus ⎬ "Micro-evolution"
Species ⎭

At the bottom of the scale there is admittedly a certain fluidity and plasticity, but this really doesn't help the theory of evolution very much.

Why? Because, the fact is, the only scientific *knowledge*—as opposed to speculation—we have of mutations is that they seldom if ever result in new traits in any organism. In fact, most mutations are harmful to the organism. Among humans we usually call them "birth defects," like sickle cell anemia. Evolutionists have searched among genetic mutations for decades, trying to produce a new animal, but they always end up with the same basic animal they started with. You can bombard fruit flies with radioactivity and get all kinds of weird variations, many of them harmful, but you still end up with a fruit fly.

Thus far the evidence seems to indicate that unbridgable genetic barriers, unbridgable breeding gaps exist between distinct kinds of animals. This is a serious problem with general evolution because its adherents must produce evidence to indicate that evolution has taken place "from amoeba to man" or "from molecules to man." So far, there is no solid scientific evidence from genetics for this theory.

Ordinary people, laymen if you please, have this strange belief that scientists constantly do laboratory work that turns out incontrovertible proof for evolution. This isn't true now, nor has it ever been true. Evolution is still an open question now, as it was in Darwin's day. No big knockout blow against creation has been delivered from any laboratory on earth.

THE REAL PROOF: FOSSIL REMAINS

It doesn't take long in one's study of the evidence

for evolution to see that the crucial data lie in the fossil record. As Sir Julian Huxley said, if you can't prove evolution there, then all the other arguments are very weak. The fossil record shows that various animal forms once existed which are now extinct and it seems to suggest that in certain cases there has been a gradual development of anatomical structures through successive stages from simple to complex. The evidence of fossils is *good enough* to force the creationist to give up his position that there have been no changes since the creation, an idea that some creationists maintain but which is not at all required by Scripture.

There can be no doubt that many life forms have become extinct since the creation, for example, the dinosaurs. Anyone who seriously suggests that the devil planted dinosaur bones in the earth to test the faith of believers makes the creationist position look ridiculous. What the evolutionist must see, however, is that the Bible nowhere says that we have an absolutely frozen creation since God made everything. Genesis 1 teaches only the general fixity of kinds of animals; it doesn't say that some types would never die out. Nowhere does Scripture require us to believe in a totally static creation, since, as noted earlier, we really don't know what "kind" meant in the creation narrative. New species may and probably do arise.

However, before anyone bows down and worships the fossil record as adequate proof of evolution, we do well to point out certain problems with this piece of evidence.

(1) First, we must realize how very sketchy, damaged, and incomplete the fossil record really is. Perhaps the greatest problem facing the paleontologist is that he has only the skeletal system to work with. He must reconstruct the rest of the animal's structure from the skeleton. But the skeleton can be drastically altered by things like dietary deficiencies, rickets, and pituitary giantism, making it even more difficult to reconstruct and classify the organism. Fossils have often been twisted and distorted by the great pressure of the rocks upon them. They are often damaged and exposed by erosion.

Fossils can easily be misinterpreted. Some species are so varied that you might never be able to see the essential features of a species just from fossil remains. For example, all dogs from the tiny Chihuahua to the St. Bernard belong to just one species, *Canis familiaris*. But if you didn't know the dog as a modern species, if you knew it only from fossilized skeletons, you might conclude that you were dealing with a number of separate species.

The fossil record is very incomplete. We have millions of fossils, true, but they represent only a fraction of the many animals that lived in the past. In addition, our existing fossils aren't a true random sample of the types that have lived before. Most of our fossils are over-represented by organisms from shallow seas, swampy areas, river mouths, and bogs.

You get some idea of how sketchy the fossil evidence is if you'll imagine the D. A. standing up in court and saying, "Ladies and gentlemen of the jury, most of the evidence for the defendant's guilt comes from his house, but unfortunately his house just burned down."

(2) Second, the geological column containing fossil remains isn't the same all over the earth. Nowhere on earth do you find a perfect column all the way from the earliest animal deposits to the present. If you did, it would be about one hundred miles deep (our best example, the Grand Canyon, is only one mile deep). Those neat little complete charts you see in the science textbooks are *theoretical reconstructions*. They aren't based on any *observed* reality.

Moreover, the geological layers are often all scrambled up with each other. Sometimes you find layers supposed to be recent lying right down on the "basement complex," the—alleged—bottom of the series. Sometimes layers that are supposed to be millions of years apart are found right next to each other, with no apparent reason how they got that way. If evolution is a fact, it's strange why we can't find a single case of a complete or even near-complete example of the geological column.

(3) Third, dating has always been a problem when scientists deal with the fossil remains and the geological column. Certainly if evolution is to be taught as fact it needs a much more precise method of dating.

One of the most indefensible dating methods is

using the "index fossil" to establish the date of a certain geological stratum. Such scientists just blandly *assume* the theory of evolution and then argue that only one group of species can be living at any one time. Thus, when they discover in the rocks of a certain geological layer certain animal and plant species they jump to the conclusion that that layer has the same date as the animals and plants had in the— alleged—evolutionary column.

But anyone, even a layman, can see that you must know the age of the fossils *before* you can say anything about the age of the rocks. Otherwise you are clearly reasoning in a circle; you date the fossils by the rocks and then date the rocks by the fossils! This unscrupulous reasoning has been scored by more than one scientist. R. H. Rastall wrote in *Encyclopedia Britannica* (X, 168):

> It cannot be denied from a strictly philosophical standpoint geologists are here arguing in a circle. The succession of organisms has been determined by a study of their remains embedded in the rocks, and the relative ages of the rocks are determined by the remains of organisms that they contain.

All evolutionists must answer this question: is there an accurate, independent method of dating either the rocks or the fossils without thus reasoning in a circle? If we mean a method of dating that has no problems and that enjoys general acceptance by scientists, then the answer is *no.* All of the known methods have problems.

Carbon-14, the best known dating process, is almost useless in testing the evolutionary hypothesis, because it begins to accumulate a margin of error as it goes back past about 2000 B. C. Scientists have established this by comparing C-14 with tree ring dating, whose margin of error is almost nil. C-14 has almost no reliability at all past 40,000 B. C. One professional dating company in Cambridge, Massachusetts, won't date anything that shows a date prior to about 1000 B.C.

All dating methods that use the decay of radioactive elements (uranium, thorium, potassium, rubidium) are based on two assumptions:

(a) that these chemicals have always decayed at a constant rate and

(b) that the rocks containing these chemicals have never been contaminated.

At first it may seem reasonable to grant that the rate of decay has always been the same, yet we can never be certain. All these elements have a very slow rate of decay and if, for some unknown reason, the rate of decay was faster or slower when the universe was younger it would upset all our computations.

It's interesting that some scientists will assert a Big Bang Theory, which postulates an incredible modification of matter's behavior at the origin of the cosmos, but will then demand that all behavior since that time be perfectly uniform! Of course, I can understand the strong motive for wanting uniformitarianism to be true—all the known dating methods are suspect if it isn't true.

The second assumption, that the rocks containing radioactive elements have never been contaminated, is even more difficult to grant. Many scientists point out, correctly, that rocks are not perfectly sealed off from their environment. Rocks "breathe in" certain chemicals through the ages; they are permeated by oxygen, water, and carbon dioxide. Thus, it would be remarkable if their chemical constitution remained perfectly static for millions or billions of years.

None of this is cause for alarm—unless you're teaching a theory as fact that is based on the assumption of exact dating methods.

(4) Fourth, the fossil record reveals something that is disturbing to the evolutionary theory. It shows that complex animals appear rather suddenly in the early strata. In the oldest rocks, the Cambrian, we find examples of almost all the major phyla of animals existing in the world today. There are more than five thousand species in the Cambrian strata and the most striking thing about them is that they are complex, not simple.

For example, in the Cambrian rocks we find lamp shells, moss animals, worms, trilobites, and shrimp. These creatures have complex organs: intestines, stomachs, bristles, spines, and appendages. They have eyes and feelers, which indicates that they possessed a good nervous system. They have gills, which shows that they both extracted oxygen from the water and had complex blood circulation systems. Some of these Cambrian fossils grew by molting, a complicated process still not thoroughly understood by scientists. They had intricate mouthpieces to strain special foods out of the water. Nothing primitive or simple about these Cambrian creatures!

Now the big question: *where are the ancestors of these Cambrian fossils?* We find no organisms with partially-formed intestines, stomachs, bristles, spines, appendages, eyes, feelers, and gills. Where are all the simpler creatures that should have led up to these complex forms—if "molecules to man" evolution is supposed to be a scientific fact? This problem is so acute that even Darwin himself admitted that it "may truly be urged as a valid argument" against evolution. Darwin hoped that more fossils would turn up these ancestors of the Cambrians, but a century later they are still missing.

Sometimes evolutionists ask creationists: "Can you produce clear-cut evidence that definitely suggests creation? Can you indicate some material that can *only* be explained by creation?" Of course, this is an unfair demand, and would kill evolution as well as creation, but I venture to suggest that a good sign of creation would be *the appearance of something without antecedents.* Doesn't the sudden appearance of these Cambrian animals with no antecedents suggest creation rather than evolution? We may state it in syllogistic form this way:

1. If evolution has occurred, we would find antecedents.
2. We find no antecedents.
3. Therefore, evolution hasn't occurred.[1]

Anyone familiar with the rules of the hypothetical syllogism will see that this argument uses a valid operation: denying the consequent. Of course, the soundness of the argument depends on the truth of the first premise. It's possible, I admit, that evolution has occurred and that for some strange reason the antecedents have disappeared. But the evolutionist should try to give us a plausible reason why they disappeared and he should certainly stop dogmatizing about his theory in view of these missing antecedents.

(5) Fifth, and finally, the fossil record reveals something else missing that disturbs evolution. It shows that there are few, if any, transitional forms between the great groups of animals. These "missing links" also are missing in animals that are alive today. In fact, the gaps in the fossil record correspond closely to the gaps we have between animal and plant groups today.

For instance, nearly all new categories above the level of *family* (order, class, phylum) appear in the fossil record suddenly and are not led up to by any gradual, completely continuous, transitional forms.

---

1. The kind of syllogism used here is the hypothetical syllogism, where you reason, "if . . . then." The first part of your premise is called the *antecedent* and the second part the *consequent*.

There is a big lacuna from protozoa to metazoa, from fish to amphibians, from amphibians to reptiles, from reptiles to birds and mammals, and from invertebrates to vertebrates. If gills became lungs and fins became legs and scales became feathers then why is it that we find no transitional forms that combine features of both types of creatures?

Ever since Darwin, scientists have been searching for these "missing links," which have become a kind of Holy Grail for the evolutionists. But a century has passed and the links are still missing. Surely enough fossils have been unearthed in the last century to prove that they will never be found. The evolutionist might as well accept that fact and get down to explaining why there are no transitional forms.

Many evolutionists say that transitional forms were so few and so unusual that they left no fossil remains. They argue that the origins of every group necessarily disappear and it is only when a phylum has become well established that we can expect it to leave any fossil remains.

Now this really sounds like special pleading! Isn't it convenient for the theory that all the transitional forms disappeared? It's very difficult to believe that the transitions were accomplished so quickly and through such a small number of organisms. Can you give any good reason why this happened just this way? If evolution was a gradual process then the transitional forms must also have been gradual. There should be some evidence of these transitions in the fossil record, but very few forms have ever been found, and curious battles occur over some of the ones that have been found.[2] We have no trace of half-wings or half-legs or any other nascent organ among the fossil remains.

We must conclude, then, that the fossil record is not exactly an open-and-shut case for evolution. The fossil record has to be interpreted and once we interpret it we find that evolution is only one possible reading of the bones. Maybe we should do as Voltaire suggested and just put down at the bottom of this investigation the two letters Roman judges used in a moot case, NL, for *non liquet,* "It is not clear."

WHAT ABOUT THE CREATION OF LIFE?

In recent years many people, even many Christians, have developed a deep fear that scientists will someday create life in the laboratory, thereby prove evolution, and then "it'll all be over for the theist." This fear is based on a misunderstanding not only of the scientific method but also of what Christianity teaches about God and His relationship to the world.

The error involved here is the notion that if man

---

2. Most evolutionists will jump at a possible missing link, *Archaeopteryx,* a fossil that is supposed to combine lizardlike and birdlike traits. However, most ornithologists say *Archaeopteryx* is just a bird, not a transitional form. It's strange that such a battle rages around even the few missing links we have.

explains everything, he has expelled God from the cosmos. The idea is that, "If we can't use God to explain something then we'll have to kick Him out." Many people think that man has explained everything else but the creation of life. That is somehow sacred and in some way a special act of God. This view is encouraged by the mechanist who claims that when science finally creates life, then his mechanistic naturalism, his materialistic determinism will be proved once and for all. It's almost like a countdown, nine . . . eight . . . seven . . . in a few decades God will self-destruct.

But, both the fearful Christian and the hopeful mechanist are wrong. If science should happen to create life—and it certainly hasn't yet—that will prove almost nothing about the problem of origins. Three points will make this clear.

(1) First, man can never really *create* life, as God created the universe. Man can only *synthesize* life. He may someday be able to arrange the conditions from which life will arise, but that wouldn't be creation. When religious people speak of creation they mean creation *ex nihilo*, "creation out of nothing." God made the cosmos out of nothing; *that* was true creation. If man synthesizes life it will be from previously existing chemicals.

(2) Now that we have our terminology straight, we note, second, that synthesis of life won't prove evolution. What rational man accomplishes deliberately right now tells us nothing about what non-rational

nature might have accidentally done in the past. I know you may get tired of hearing this point, but let me assure you, I get tired of having to make it to the person who concludes too much from some current experiment!

The fact is, there is *no such thing* as a scientific view of the origin of life and the universe. No one was there to observe when life originated and so no one can dogmatize about how it happened. You may perform an experiment today and speculate that it might have happened that way in the past, but this is not a scientific conclusion. You could never devise an experiment to prove what happened in the past. You may believe in spontaneous generation if you like, but don't call it science and don't teach it as science.

As noted earlier, you can duplicate or reproduce something done in the past, but that doesn't prove how it was done in the first instance of its appearance. With modern tools we could duplicate exactly the huge stone monoliths of Easter Island, but that wouldn't necessarily prove anything about how the Easter Islanders first produced them.

(3) Third, according to the Christian view of God, creation, and the nature of man, it is very likely that man will someday synthesize life. The Bible teaches that man was made in the image of God (Gen. 1:26, 27; 9:6; Ps. 8:6-8; James 3:9). We feel that man's attributes, such as *intelligence, personality, freedom, morality,* and *aesthetic appreciation* are part of God's

image in him. Part of that image we also believe to be the *capacity to create.*

Now, if man's intelligence has its roots in God's intelligence, and if God made life from inert chemicals, it shouldn't surprise us that man might someday discover the same life formula. Is the synthesis of life really any different from some of the other startling scientific breakthroughs in history, e.g. the discovery of atomic power? I once knew some people who thought that if man ever got to the moon it would be the end of the Christian faith. Well, he got there, and those folks are still Christians.

In sum, to argue that God doesn't exist because man can synthesize life would be as ridiculous as arguing that Rembrandt never existed because someone had made a copy of one of his paintings.

CONCLUSION

We find, therefore, after careful examination, that the evidence for evolution is far from overwhelming. If this is the best evidence we have, then we certainly can't say evolution is the only possible or only plausible theory of origins. If I were a District Attorney and had to go into court with evidence against a man no better than this evidence evolutionists present against creationism, I would be afraid that the jury would rule, "Not guilty!"

And now—what should we teach in the public schools? Let's discuss that in the next chapter.

Chapter 4

WHAT SHOULD WE TEACH?

If our reasoning up to this point has been correct, it follows that the problem of origins is still an open question. We can't close the question in favor of evolution, because the evidence isn't strong enough. In case this matter is still a bit fuzzy for some readers, we can approach the problem from another angle. This requires us to discuss another fallacy, a key one in understanding the scientific method.

THE FALLACY OF ASSERTING THE CONSEQUENT

In 1973 I participated in a debate with an evolutionist at the University of California, Davis. We got into a vigorous discussion on the spontaneous generation of life from inert chemicals. When one student asked the evolutionist, "But how do you know it really happened?" this scientist replied: "Well, we're here, aren't we?" This answer commits the fallacy of *asserting the consequent*. The argument runs like this:

1. If spontaneous generation of life occurred, then we would be here.
2. We are here.
3. Therefore, spontaneous generation of life has occurred.

One can see that the creationist could make the same argument with equal force:

1. If creation occurred, we would be here.
2. We are here.
3. Therefore, creation has occurred.

In other words, we would be here regardless of which occurred—creation or evolution. Asserting the consequent is a fallacy, therefore, because you can't always tell how many different causes there are of a given result or consequent. For instance, if you reasoned . . .

1. If it rains, then I'll get wet.
2. I am wet.
3. Therefore, it has rained.

. . . that would be fallacious because there are many ways of getting wet. The simple fact that you're wet doesn't prove that it has rained.

It's a curious fact that the scientific method must use this operation—asserting the consequent—when it tries to confirm any theory. There's nothing wrong in asserting the consequent *if* (a big if!) you keep researching and keep experimenting to try to show that the antecedent, the theory you're testing, is *the only possible cause* of the consequent. If you can prove this, then your proposition would become an "if-and-only-if" proposition. It would obviously be valid:

1. If and only if evolution occurred would we be here.
2. We are here.
3. Therefore, evolution has occurred.

There are no fallacious operations in the hypothetical syllogism if you have an if-and-only-if first premise. But, as you can readily imagine, such premises are exceedingly rare. In actual practice, you almost never meet one, because it's nearly impossible to eliminate all the possible causes except one. As we saw in chapter three, the evolutionist certainly hasn't proved that evolution is the only possible explanation of the material in the case. We noticed that creation can explain some of the same data just as easily or better than evolution.

You can see this fallacy at work in the history of science, e.g. in the province of chemistry. By the end of the seventeenth century chemistry was slowly becoming a bona fide science. In its search for general laws to govern the various transformations of matter, some early chemists came up with an interesting hypothesis called "the Phlogiston Theory." The principal sponsors of this theory were Johann Joachim Becher (1635-82), a physician and alchemist, and Georg Ernst Stahl (1660-1734), a professor of medicine at the University of Halle. In 1702 Stahl introduced the word "phlogiston," which comes from the Greek for "inflammable."

The phlogiston theory postulated a hypothetical material that chemists believed to be present in all combustible substances. Chemists claimed that this material accounted not only for combustion reactions but also for the rusting of iron. They thought that when a fuel was burned phlogiston escaped, leaving the other components of the material behind, like ash. They explained the rusting of iron as phlogiston escaping more slowly.

This theory had several problems, but it was amazing how chemists were able to get around the problems with certain modifications of the basic theory. Even great investigators like Henry Cavendish and Joseph Priestly accounted for their results in the studies of hydrogen and oxygen by using the phlogiston theory. What was so strange was that the very chemists who did the most to overthrow the theory did it unwittingly, because their experiments were conducted with the theory as the initial assumption.

The great French chemist, Antoine Laurent Lavoisier (1743-94) completely disproved the theory in 1785-89. His new theories so smoothly accounted for both the known facts and the problems of phlogiston that no one has believed in phlogiston since. But it's interesting that for so long a time this completely erroneous theory apparently covered all the known facts and even advanced the progress of chemistry during the heyday of its domination. We can be sure that some champion of phlogiston argued:

1. If phlogiston exists, then iron will rust.
2. Iron does rust.
3. Therefore, phlogiston exists.

The case of phlogiston should give us fair warning: don't count your theories before you've definitely eliminated all other possible explanations. Certainly you shouldn't teach a theory as absolute fact until some definitive evidence has eliminated all of its rivals.

But we still teach only evolution. Why? Is there any justification for this? The evolutionist has two final arguments we must now consider.

ARGUMENTUM AD IGNORANTIAM

Evolutionists sometimes argue: "Well, since creation can't be established, therefore evolution wins by default." This idea of any theory "winning by default" is the essence of *Argumentum ad Ignorantiam,* "an argument addressed to ignorance." You commit this fallacy when you reason that since one position can't prove itself the other wins by default. This is a logical error for two reasons.

(1) First, before you can win by default, you must prove that there are only two possible theories. There may be a third or a fourth possibility. It would be silly for one combatant to shout, "I win!", when he

has eliminated only one alternative theory and others are waiting to enter the contest.

But, you object, haven't we really got only two theories on this matter of origins—creation and evolution? Wouldn't the failure to establish creation prove evolution?

(2) No, because even if I grant that we have only two theories, the failure to prove one doesn't prove the other, *unless* you have some *independent* evidence to support the second theory. If creation isn't proved—we grant this for the sake of the point—then it might be that we should just suspend judgment, not opt for evolution. The most you can conclude is that, at present, we have insufficient data for making a choice between creation and evolution.

Take this example: there is either life on Mars or there isn't. So far, we haven't found any life on Mars. Should we conclude, then, that there is no life on Mars? No, because there could still be life on Mars and we just haven't discovered it yet. To argue otherwise would be fallacious.[1]

---

1. Norman Macbeth sees this point well in his *Darwin Retired—An Appeal to Reason* (Boston: Gambit, 1971), pp. 5-7. He points out, correctly, that when a man propounds a theory he's obligated to support every link in the chain of his reasoning, while, conversely, a critic or skeptic may peck away at any aspect of the theory, testing it for flaws. The critic isn't obligated to set up any theory of his own or offer any alternate theory; he can be purely negative if he wants to. "If a theory conflicts with the facts or with reason," writes Macbeth, "it is entitled to no respect.... Whether a better theory is offered, is irrelevant."

So, if the evidence for evolution is inadequate and if it's wrong to declare a winner by default . . . why do we still teach evolution as the only theory of origins in the schools?

This leads us to another objection used by the evolutionist: "Evolution is the only theory that we could possibly verify scientifically. You could never check creation by any known empirical means. Therefore, even though it has problems, we should teach evolution and not creation in the science classes." In sum, the evolutionist claims that evolution wins by default since it is empirical and creation, by definition, is metaphysical.

First, this objection isn't entirely accurate. It's wrong to say that creation has absolutely no observable empirical results that we can check. We've noticed already that creation explains three conditions that trouble evolution—(a) the apparent fixity of animal kinds, (b) the sudden appearance of complex animals in the Cambrian strata, and (c) the missing transitional forms in the fossil record.

Second, what is more inaccurate in this argument is the suggestion that evolution has sufficient empirical verification, that it has some special knockout proof emerging daily from laboratories around the world. This simply isn't true. Forgive me for having to say it again: there is no such thing as genuine "scientific proof" or "scientific knowledge" about the past, because you can never inspect the object *directly*. You can't go back and cross the Delaware with George

Washington or conquer Gaul with Caesar. Nor can you go back and observe scales becoming feathers or wings becoming arms. Evolution suffers the same epistemological handicap as history—you must study it *indirectly.*

If evolution wins the contest by default merely because it's more empirical then we can see that our discussion has finally come full circle. We're back to Scientism again. This argument assumes that empirical verification is the only possible type of verification in all realms of knowledge. Suppose it should turn out that the truth about origins lies outside our empirical powers? Wouldn't it then be unfair to teach just the theory that could be verified empirically? To rule out creation on this ground would be like saying: "A supernatural solution to the problem of origins is impossible—by definition!" Isn't this pretty high-handed?

Who gave anyone the right to make such a rule? Who proved that the solution to the problem of origins had to be an empirical solution? If a detective announced at the very beginning of his investigation that, "Only a member of the family could have committed this crime," we would object that this was an illegitimate restriction of the possible circle of suspects. But isn't the empiricist doing this same thing when he eliminates the supernatural from his choice of solutions simply because it is supernatural?

Some evolutionists have actually said that evolution must be true "because the only other alternative,

more—of establishing Scientific Humanism or Naturalism as a state religion when we teach only evolution. People never seem to stop and think that, given the immense prestige of science in our culture, exclusively teaching evolution subtly inculcates such attitudes as scientism, empiricism, materialism, and naturalism—even while claiming to be academically neutral.

Second, we're not advocating that only creation be taught in science classes. We want no return to pre-Scopes days. We advocate simply that creation be taught as an alternative theory of origins, with as much power to correlate and explain the data as evolution. If origins is still an open question, it would actually improve the student's understanding of the scientific method to present both models and discuss how both seek to correlate the data we discussed in chapter three.

I really doubt that the Founding Fathers were intending to give a definition of the scientific method when they wrote the First Amendment. The argument that teaching creation violates the First Amendment assumes that the Founding Fathers favored an exclusively empirical process of verification, which, if true, would destroy most of their own political accomplishments.

Here's an interesting question: Could the public schools teach a simple moral precept like, "Love your neighbor"? This precept is taught by several world religions—can we teach it in the schools? If so, then it follows that teaching what is found in a religion doesn't necessarily violate the First Amendment.

But can altruism be verified empirically? Can you prove love in the laboratory? "Oh, but love is obvious," you reply. "All people agree on love. But creation is metaphysical and controversial."

Really? Don't be too sure! The Nazis didn't think love was so obvious. Friedrich Nietzsche said love was nonsense, the ethic of the herd, the excuse of weak people. Hitler said, "The conscience is a Jewish invention, a blemish like circumcision." If you get into a deep discussion with a moral relativist or an ethical nihilist on the subject of altruism you'll discover that love can be as controversial and speculative as creation.

The fact is, we teach a lot of things in our public schools—love, democracy, integrity—that are metaphysical, axiological, speculative, open to question, things we could never verify by empiricism. By what logical rule, then, do we keep out the teaching of creation?

Chapter 5 | SOCIAL DARWINISM and the GENETIC FALLACY

Evolutionists sometimes feel that we creationists have an irrational, knee-jerk reaction to the theory of evolution. They feel that our opposition is more emotional than rational. I think by now the reader will have to conclude that we have a reasonable basis for objecting to the teaching of evolution as fact—namely, the evidence is weak.

But I personally must admit that, in addition to rational arguments, I have strong emotional misgivings about the theory of evolution. As Mark Twain once said, "I'm prejudiced on this topic and I'd be ashamed if I weren't!" As an European historian, I've been able to see the doleful effects of the application of the theory over the last century. In this chapter, I'd like to explain a little further why Christians become so alarmed over "Social Darwinism," the application of Darwinian evolution to human affairs. In the process, we'll look at yet another fallacy, the Genetic Fallacy.

THE ANATOMY OF SOCIAL DARWINISM

Evolution per se merely claims that life developed slowly from the simple to the complex, that all life is interconnected, that the later, more intricate forms emerged out of the earlier, simpler forms. Darwin came along and added the theory which explained the mechanism, the "how" of evolution: *Natural selection from accidental variations.*

Darwin argued that all forms of life struggle for existence; they fight over the earth's available food. In this struggle there must be some winners and some losers. The strong and swift eliminate the weak and slow; they survive to pass on special new features to their offspring. This "survival of the fittest" (not Darwin's phrase) automatically guarantees that variations favoring survival will be preserved.

Darwinian evolution, therefore, rules out God, or Spirit, or Providence, or Life Force, or any other outside force to explain the evolution of life on Earth. Darwin could say, as the French scientist Laplace said to Napoleon: "Sire, I have no need of that hypothesis." Jacques Barzun writes: "Exaggerating for the sake of brevity, one could interpret Darwinism as meaning that the whole of animal evolution had taken place among absolute robots, which reproduced their kind with slight, purposeless variations of form."[1]

Social Darwinism comes into play when thinkers uncritically apply the principle of natural selection to the problems of human society. Darwinism in sociology leads to a vulgar justification of ruthless competition, struggle, brutality, and violence among men. Let's look at some historical incarnations of Darwinism.

(1) Laissez-faire capitalists used Darwinism to defend their system of unrestrained competition in the business world of the late nineteenth century. In England, disciples of Adam Smith such as Herbert Spencer argued against poor relief and all forms of social welfare by appeal to the doctrine of survival. In America, John D. Rockefeller argued that the growth of a large business was merely the survival of the fittest. "The American Beauty Rose," he said, "can be produced in the splendor and fragrance which brings cheer to its beholder only by sacrificing the early buds which grow up around it. This is not an evil tendency in business. It is merely the working out of a law of nature and a law of God."[2]

---

1. Jacques Barzun, *Darwin, Marx, Wagner: Critique of a Heritage* (Garden City, N. Y.: Doubleday, 1958), p. 11.

2. See Richard Olson, ed., *Science as Metaphor: The Historical Role of Scientific Theories in Forming Western Culture* (Belmont, Ca.: Wadsworth, 1971), p. 111. For two excellent studies see Richard Hofstadter, *Social Darwinism in American Thought, 1816-1915* (Philadelphia: University of Pennsylvania Press, 1944) and Harold Y. Vanderpoor, ed., *Darwin and Darwinism* (Lexington, Mass.: Heath, 1973).

George Nasmyth spoke accurately when he charged that, "The new 'Social Darwinism' was seized upon with enthusiasm by all men of violence because it permitted them to raise the basest instincts of greed and vandalism to the height of a universal law of nature."[3]

(2) Imperialists used Darwinism to justify the conquest and exploitation of non-western peoples in the last century. They exhorted their compatriots to "take up the white man's burden" and carry the blessings of western civilization to the "inferior" dark-skinned peoples of the globe. Many ruling classes of the western countries denied rights to their less educated subjects simply on the grounds that they weren't sufficiently evolved.

The history of European nations from 1870 to 1914 is largely one of competition for rival empires. England and France expanded their already considerable holdings in Africa and Asia. In the same period, Germany, Italy, Belgium, and Portugal entered into the competition of the new imperialism. Russia, already on the move for centuries, expanded farther to the Pacific. Japan pushed into Formosa and Korea. The United States expanded to the Pacific and then annexed Hawaii and the Philippines. All of this imper-

---

3. George Nasmyth, *Social Progress and the Darwinism Theory: A Study of Force as a Factor in Human Relations* (New York: G. P. Putnam's Sons, 1916), ch. 2.

ialism, justified by Darwinian evolution, was a potent factor in bringing on the Great War of 1914.[4]

In fairness, one must note that you can't blame Charles Darwin personally for all this "social" Darwinism, any more than you can blame Newton for the Social Newtonism of the eighteenth century Enlightenment. But Darwin's theory *did* obscure the vital difference between man and all other animals and this led to the mistakes of the Social Darwinians.

For example, while speculating on the changes necessary to turn a "native" into a civilized man, Darwin remarked that we would have to wait for him to evolve farther, because civilization was a function of biology. This is obviously incorrect, as we now know, and as many people knew before the theory of evolution became fashionable. Even Francis Bacon, writing 250 years earlier than Darwin, knew better than this. Speaking of the native American Indians, Bacon said, "Consider the abyss which separates the life of men in some highly civilized region of Europe from that of some savage, barbarous tract of New India. So great is it that one might appear a god to the other. . . . And this is the effect not of soil, not of climate, not of physique, *but of the arts.*"[5] In sum, Bacon knew that civilization was a function of society, not of biology.

---

4. See Hannah Arendt, *The Origins of Totalitarianism,* 2nd enlarged ed. (New York, 1958), pp. 124ff.

5. Cited in B. Farrington, *What Darwin Really Said* (New York: Schocken Books, 1966), p. 104. Italics mine.

(3) Exponents of war used Darwinism to justify military struggle among nations. Only the stern test of combat, militarists insisted, could reveal which nation was stronger than another. Nature shows us, they said, that war is the great winnowing process, the terrible final examination between nations. The great German general, von Moltke, summed it up well: "Eternal peace is just a dream, and not a very pretty one at that."

By a curious accident, a crucial, decisive war was fought in the very year that Darwin's second book, *The Descent of Man,* appeared. In 1870-71 Prussia and France carried on a short but decisive conflict that ended with Prussia the obvious victor. The German people lost no time in drawing the proper Darwinian conclusions about the war and quickly dubbed themselves the "fittest"—since they had "survived."

And what did the French do? Paradoxically, the vanquished nation, instead of condemning the vulgar new worship of success, instead of shouting, "Long live justice!", jumped on the Darwinian bandwagon and screamed, "Might is right!" along with the Germans. They began preparing for a war of revenge.

It's well for us to remember that sentiments such as these were held, not only by ordinary people, but also by eminent scholars and scientists. For example, sociologist Karl Pearson argued that a vigorous race could keep its capacities up to a high pitch of efficiency only by contest, "chiefly by way of war with inferior races, and with equal races by the struggle for trade routes and for the sources of raw material and of food supply." Pearson concluded pompously, "This is the natural history view of mankind, and I do not think you can in its main features subvert it."[6]

The American novelist, Jack London, expressed this idea in very appropriate terms. Said Wolf Larsen:

> One man cannot wrong another man. He can only wrong himself. As I see it, I do wrong always when I consider the interests of others. Don't you see? How can two particles of yeast wrong each other by striving to devour each other? It is their inborn heritage to strive to devour, and to strive not to be devoured. When they depart from this, they sin.[7]

So! Humans are to act like two particles of yeast. We note again the confusion between the human and the nonhuman. Two mindless, amoral yeast particles struggling to devour—this is Darwinian man.

(4) Champions of eugenics used Darwinism to push for eugenics legislation. Eugenics (literally, "good breeding") is the science of breeding applied to human beings. If we can improve animals by selective breeding, it was argued, why not also humans? Eugenics proponents usually called for laws to promote mating the fit with the fit and forbidding the mating of fit with unfit. Thus, state manipulation of mating would someday produce a "higher type of

---

6. Cited in Olson, *Science as Metaphor,* p. 140.

7. Jack London, *Sea Wolf* (New York: Macmillan, 1931), p. 79.

man." They called for laws to sterilize people with hereditary diseases harmful to society. They argued that only a rigorous, ruthless process of selection, involving both extermination and deliberate breeding, could prevent faulty lines of evolution and insure the superiority of one race or nation over another.

Eugenics champions tended to be very critical of all forms of altruistic morality, toleration, humanitarianism, liberalism, democracy, or internationalism, because these sentiments, with their concern for the unfit, were "counterselective." Nature wipes out the weak specimen; shouldn't sound legislation do the same?[8]

(5) Racists found Darwinism especially useful in preaching their gospel of ethnic superiority. Racism asserts that the human family is hopelessly fractionalized and that the "fractions"—the distinct races—have varying values. Racism asserts that struggle, not cooperation, is the normal, yea even the desirable, state of race relations and that competition proves some races superior to others in intelligence, creativity, and cultural capacity. "Without universal conflict," Herbert Spencer claimed, "there would have been no development of the active powers."

The ideology of Nazi Germany combined many of these Social Darwinian features just discussed—

---

8. For a look at this strain in Hitler's background, see Joachim C. Fest, *Hitler,* trans. Richard and Clara Winston (New York: Random House, 1975), p. 54.

notably racism, imperialism, militarism, and eugenics. As Hitler's biographer, Alan Bullock, said, the core of Nazi ideology was a "crude Social Darwinism." Hitler stated:

Man has become great through struggle. . . . Whatever goal man has reached is due to his originality plus his brutality. . . . All life is bound up in these three theses: Struggle is the father of all things, virtue lies in blood, leadership is primary and decisive.

Hitler took his cue from Nietzsche, who had insisted that since God is dead altruism is also dead, because altruism is based on theism. Hitler agreed that altruism or love is "counterselective." "The whole work of nature," he insisted, "is a mighty struggle between strength and weakness—an eternal victory of the strong over the weak." Any person or state that offends this elementary law will fail. "Only force rules. Force is the first law." But what about morality? "History proves," concluded Hitler, "he who has not the strength—him the 'right in itself' profits not a whit."[9]

When the Nazis finally got down to putting this racism into actual legislation, they spelled out what they considered the logical implications of evolution. In the infamous Nuremberg Laws (1935), directed principally against the Jews, they asserted that "there is a greater difference between the lowest forms still

9. Alan Bullock, *Hitler: A Study in Tyranny* (New York: Bantam Books, 1964), pp. 345-46.

called human and our superior races [Aryan] than between the lowest man and monkeys of the highest order." In other words, the Jews and Slavs, because they were vastly inferior to Aryans, were closer to apes than to their fellow humans!

Mortimer Adler states the issue here with precision when he asks:

> What was wrong *in principle* with the Nazi policies toward the Jews and Slavs . . . if the only psychological differences between men and other animals are differences in degree? What is wrong *in principle* with the actions of enslavers through human history who justified their ownership and use of men as chattel on the ground that the enslaved were inferiors (barbarians, gentiles, untouchables, "natural slaves, fit only for use")?[10]

Perhaps now the evolutionist will understand a little better why religious people are disturbed by certain implications of the classical naturalistic theory of Darwinian evolution. Jesus warned us that we could know something by its fruit (Matt. 7:16). When we see such evil fruit falling on the ground we're naturally inclined to examine the philosophical tree very carefully.

THE GENETIC FALLACY

But what is the Genetic Fallacy and how does

---

10. Mortimer Adler, *The Difference of Man and the Difference it Makes* (New York: Holt, Rinehard and Winston, 1967), p. 264.

Darwinism commit this logical error? This fallacy is a special form of the Reductive Fallacy, which, as you recall, is reducing a complex entity to only one of its many aspects. You commit the Genetic Fallacy when you claim that something is "merely" or "nothing but" its *genesis* (its origins), or when you demean or belittle something just because of its humble or inauspicious beginnings. This fallacy overlooks the patent fact of human experience that many great and wonderful things in life begin in very humble ways.

For example, a man starts out as a single fertilized ovum. But it would be ridiculous for you to walk up to a fifty-year old man and say, "You're nothing but a fertilized ovum walking around!" A man's origins, no matter how unspectacular, prove nothing about his present state. Something that can grow, change and improve is obviously going to outrun its origins; any observation made of it must correspond to its present status, not its *beginnings.*

Darwinism argues that since man *began* as an animal, he isn't much more than an animal now, just a very complex animal. Certainly the same laws that apply to animal behavior, like natural selection, must be applied to man too. Darwinians fail to see that with man you reach a new rung on the ladder of life, a psycho-social dimension that separates man from the animals by a great gulf. Mental and social development in man is a new process, one that can't be explained by mere biological mechanisms. Therefore, any analogy between biological and sociological processes is misleading.[11]

Hence, the basic error of Social Darwinism is to overlook this crucial difference between human powers of reason and morality and animal instincts. No evolutionist has yet given a satisfactory explanation of how a *social instinct*, which some animals have, developed into a *social conscience*, which man alone has. Animal instincts are biologically inherited patterns of behavior. They are carried out automatically without conscious purpose. Human morality is something very different. There is no gene for morality. You don't inherit an ethical code through biological mechanisms. You might say that culture and ethics are "trans-genetic." Go back as far as you wish in human history and you find that man always governs himself by complex codes of behavior, codes which aren't instinctive or genetically inherited.[12]

---

11. We should mention here that another fallacy committed by Darwinism is *Misuse of Analogy*. As Herbert Spencer was wont to do, Darwinians talk about struggle between animals and then—without any transition or explanation—blandly assume that the very same laws are true for all human communities.

12. One of the finest presentations of evidence for the uniqueness of man is Sir Julian Huxley's *The Uniqueness of Man* (London: Chatto and Windus, 1943). See also Adler, *Difference of Man*, pp. 91ff. Adler lists seven unique features that separate man from the animals: language, tools, politics, history, religion, morality, and aesthetics.

THE MORAL ARGUMENT FOR GOD

You can see the Genetic Fallacy better if you'll consider for a moment one argument for God that Christians call *The Moral Argument*. Christian apologists have used this argument for God since the time of Immanuel Kant. In a nutshell, this argument says that you must believe in God to adequately explain man's unusual moral experience. Man feels a strong compulsion to do his duty, to engage in normative conduct. You can't explain this "moral pressure" in materialistic terms. You can best explain it by postulating a transcendent realm of morality governed by an intelligent, ethical Person, God.[13]

Immediately the evolutionist jumps on this argument by pointing out that you needn't postulate God to explain man's moral experience. On the contrary, all morality is merely a gradual growth from a foundation of animal instincts. Man gradually worked out his complex ethical systems by living together for thousands of years in social communities.

Here is a classic example of the Genetic Fallacy. When the evolutionist affirms that morality is *nothing more* than a development from animal instincts he thinks he has destroyed its objective, binding quality;

13. For a brief presentation of this argument see my *Dear Agnos: A Defense of Christianity* (Grand Rapids, Mich.: Baker, 1976), pp. 82ff. See also Elton Trueblood, *Philosophy of Religion* (1967; reprint ed., Grand Rapids, Mich.: Baker, 1975), ch. 8.

he has drained all its transcendent or mystical or authoritative aspects. He has thrown it into the same box as the appendix and the tonsils.

But notice: That's a two-edged sword he's wielding! If morality just merely evolved, then what right does the evolutionist have to upbraid me for not accepting his theory? Why does he say, "You *should* accept evolution because it's the truth"? If morality has evolved, then the value judgment he's just expressed *(we should accept the truth)* also "just evolved" in human experience. If that's true, why should we get so worked up about it? How can the evolutionist justify using the word *"should"*? According to him, all morality, all shoulds and oughts, will probably turn out to be a vestigial organ like the appendix. This is close to what Hitler thought.

Furthermore, the other side of this sword cuts off something else. *This same argument destroys reason.* Most evolutionists value reason but they contend that the human intellect developed from the physical brain of the primates. The mind once didn't exist and then supposedly evolved under the stimulus of struggle. Yet, despite this humble origin, reason is still trustworthy. If not, what was it that just framed this objection? What was it that constructed the theory of evolution? But if the mind merits our trust, even though it has evolved from lower forms, why not also trust the moral nature?

We must remember that when we talk about reason and morality we're dealing with what can be called "the authority-faculties." If we can't trust reason, then all our *thinking* is under suspicion. If we can't trust the moral faculty, then all our *ethical judgments* are thrown into question; Hitler's Final Solution has no more horror or meaning than an afternoon thunderstorm. The fact is, Darwinian evolution tends to belittle both reason and morality by merging both back into their—alleged—animal origins and obscuring their uniqueness. This was why Social Darwinians could so easily preach a gospel of struggle and espouse a code of violence.

Francis Schaeffer uses a timely analogy to make this point. Suppose, he says, that a fish is swimming in its natural element, water, and then suddenly by blind chance it develops lungs. With lungs in water the fish would be unable to live and fulfill its customary function. Would the fish be higher or lower with its new lungs? Obviously lower, because it would drown. Now, in like manner, what about man, who just accidentally develops reason, morality, aesthetics, verbal communication, purpose, and significance? Is man higher or lower on the scale of creatures? He is lower! "The green moss on the rock is higher than he," says Schaeffer, "for it can be fulfilled in the universe which exists. . . . In this situation man should not walk on the grass but respect it—for it is higher than he!"[14]

---

14. Francis A. Schaeffer, *The God Who Is There* (Downers Grove, Ill.: InterVarsity Press, 1968), p. 89.

EVOLUTION AND REASON

But let's look more closely at this problem of human reason evolving from the animals. Let us ask: "If the mind, like all else in nature, is still evolving, how can we be sure that its present structure and operation guarantee any truth?" For example, did the Law of Contradiction, the most basic law of thought, evolve like the rest of the physical body? I can't conceive of a half-formed Law of Contradiction. What could it possibly be in a half-formed state? How could it possibly function?

In epistemology, as in ethics, evolution seems to relativize everything man thinks. If the Law of Contradiction evolved, how can we be sure that there is not some new mental law, now struggling to be born, a law which will enable us to get closer to the truth about reality? Further, would this new law confirm, or contradict, evolution? Even Darwin, who wasn't much of a philosopher, dimly perceived the problem here:

> With me the horrid doubt always arises whether the convictions of man's mind, which has been developed from the minds of the lower animals, are of any value or at all trustworthy. Would anyone trust in the convictions of a monkey's mind, if there are any convictions in such a mind?[15]

---

15. Francis Darwin, ed., *Life and Letters of Charles Darwin* (1903; reprint ed., New York: Johnson Reprint, 1971), 1:285. For a good statement of the same point see C. S. Lewis, *Miracles* (New York: Macmillan, 1947), pp. 18, 32, 109.

Good question, Darwin! Why trust the convictions in anyone's brain, man or monkey? Yet we keep on trusting the secretions of man's brain. Why? Is it possible that evolutionists have more faith than they're willing to admit? Maybe they show in their actions that they really believe in the uniqueness of man, even though they deny it in their theory.

Adler puts his finger on this very inconsistency in the thinking of Sigmund Freud.[16] Freud claimed that man had the same kind of instinctual drives as the other animals. Yet man can do some unusual things to his drives: he can *divert, postpone, subdue,* and *frustrate* them. No other animal, says Freud, can so successfully master its instinctual urges. In Freudian terminology, no other animal has both civilization and its discontents.

But Freud never dealt with the crucial question implied by his own analysis of man: *where did reason come from?* If reason emerged from the instincts, where did it get this ability to *control* the instincts? Can one instinct control all the others? How? How does reason frustrate our drives? What strange new power enables it to master our pre-rational urges?

These questions cry out for an answer but no evolutionist has ever given one. The power and autonomy that Freud attributed to reason seem possible only on

16. Adler, *Difference of Man,* pp. 276ff. For the source of Freud's position see his *Civilization and its Discontents,* trans. J. Riviere (New York: Jonathan Cape and Harrison Smith, 1930).

the assumption that man is radically different from the other animals. Freud denied this assumption, but it is a key doctrine in the Christian world view. Christian theology, therefore, makes more sense of man, his origin and his unique features than naturalistic evolution does. If the evolutionary reading of man is true, then he is a profound mystery. As G. K. Chesterton said, one of the animals must have just gone off it's head!

CONCLUSION

It seems, therefore, that the unique features of man—reason, language, art, morality, religion—constitute yet another signal of creation. If the appearance of something without antecedents is a possible sign of creation (like the sudden appearance of complex animals in the Cambrian rocks), then the advent of man is a possible sign of creation. The fact that evolutionists labor to find some indications of man's unique features in the primates is tacit proof of the fact that all of us find man unique and rather hard to explain. He seems to have "emerged" without any clear antecedents.

Especially unique is man's religious capacity, a faculty definitely not found, even in embryonic form, in any other animal. Even the dedicated non-theist, Thomas Henry Huxley, confessed that, "There is a blank in the human heart and it is a God-shaped blank." What puzzles me is how a naturalist could say this and not be disturbed by the idea of a godless

nature evolving a creature with a God-shaped blank—
especially if he believed that the blank would never
be filled. Why did the purposeless, mechanical
processes of "struggle for existence" and "survival of
the fittest" produce an animal with a God-shaped
blank?

Even the most dedicated naturalistic evolutionists
agree that with man and the human mind there began
a new chapter in the history of evolving life, a
psycho-social chapter that differs sharply from all
that went before. The Christian agrees, but he adds
this proviso: The best explanation of this event is the
biblical doctrine that man was created in the image of
God.

This doesn't mean that Christians would force their
view on students in the public schools. We realize that
we can't prove such a position scientifically, in the
strictest sense of the word "scientific." But we want
the evolutionist to be honest enough to admit that he
can't prove *his* religion scientifically, either.

because I have the authority to fire you if you insist upon it!''

If evolution has no knockout evidence, if there is no overwhelming scientific proof of evolution, if spontaneous generation is highly speculative, if much of the empirical data in the question of origins is ambiguous,—if, in short, origins is still an open question—then our schools are committing this fallacy when they teach evolution exclusively. I know that not only are students often intimidated by evolutionary professors but also that biology teachers in our schools are sometimes hired and fired according to whether or not they agree with naturalistic evolution.

This is reprehensible and ought not to be tolerated in an open society or in an academic institution. As stated earlier, though the evolutionists think that teaching creation would favor a particular religion, there is abundant evidence that teaching only evolution favors Scientific Humanism. As Dr. John N. Moore of Michigan State University charges, "I hold that the late Julian Huxley and his sycophantish followers in the public schools, with their 'evolutionary' humanistic faith, are the ones who have been violating the so-called separation of church and state."[1]

---

1. Zola Levitt, *Creation: A Scientist's Choice* (Wheaton, Ill.: Victor Books, 1976), p. 72. This book is made up largely of interviews with Dr. Moore, a professor at Michigan State University who conducts a class designed to compare the two models, creation and evolution. The evolutionist side is given by a colleague who adheres to the theory of evolution.

The big question we now face is: How much longer are parents going to allow the selective indoctrination of their children—at taxpayer's expense—with an exclusive, prejudiced, anti-religious view of origins that has no genuine scientific proof? If origins is an open question and two theories are possible . . . well, I'll let you finish this last sentence.